Wrestling Greats

BILL GOLDBERG

Ross Davies

The Rosen Publishing Group, Inc.
New York

Published in 2002 by The Rosen Publishing Group, Inc.
29 East 21st Street, New York, NY 10010

Copyright © 2002 by The Rosen Publishing Group, Inc.

First Edition

All rights reserved. No part of this book may be reproduced in any form without permission in writing from the publisher, except by a reviewer.

Library of Congress Cataloging-in-Publication Data

Davies, Ross.
Bill Goldberg / by Ross Davies.— 1st ed.
p. cm. — (Wrestling greats)
Includes bibliographical references and index.
ISBN 978-1-4358-8806-7
1. Goldberg, Bill, 1966– —Juvenile literature. 2. Wrestlers—United States—Biography—Juvenile literature. [1. Goldberg, Bill, 1966–.— 2. Wrestlers.] I. Title. 2. Series.
GV1196.G65 D38 2002
796.812'092—dc21

2001002216

Manufactured in the United States of America

Contents

1 The Road to Wrestling   5
2 The Winning Streak   18
3 The Champion   33
4 The Streak Ends   44
5 Ups and Downs   63
6 The Road to Retirement   80
  Glossary   99
  For More Information   103
  For Further Reading   106
  Index   109

Bill Goldberg is one of the most accomplished and beloved wrestling stars of the past decade.

The Road to Wrestling

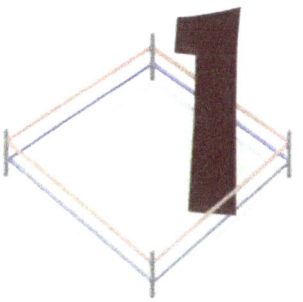

There is nothing fake about Bill Goldberg. In a sport where athletes often adopt show business names, such as Hulk Hogan, Diamond Dallas Page, Sting, and Sid Vicious, Bill Goldberg is the real thing. William Goldberg was born on December 27, 1966, in Tulsa, Oklahoma. He was the youngest of four children born to his father, Jed Goldberg, a doctor, and his mother, Ethel, a concert violinist. He has two brothers: Steve, who is twelve years older, and Mike, who is seventeen years older. He also has an older sister, Barbara.

The Goldbergs were a football-loving family living in a football-crazy state. Bill's brothers were both football stars in high school. Mike was an outstanding defensive lineman at Edison High School in Tulsa. Steve was a great linebacker and kicker at Edison High. Both were voted onto the all-state team during their high school careers and both went on to play football at the University of Minnesota.

Bill was influenced by his brothers and followed their trail to the gridiron. He started playing in eighth grade and

The Road to Wrestling

immediately gained a reputation as a hard-nosed player who hit to hurt. By the time he was fifteen, opponents feared him. "He had that snarl and love of the game, and he was born for football," said Jim Cherry, his coach at Edison High. "He was six foot three, 250 pounds with a full beard when I first saw him as a ninth grader."

Despite his ferocity on the football field, Bill always acted in a sporting manner and followed the code of ethics instilled in him by his mother and father. The code of ethics was "Do unto others as you would have them do unto you." He respected other people and never broke the rules.

With his size and athletic ability, Bill did not need to break the rules to become a star. In his senior year of high school, he was named to the all-city and all-state teams and voted defensive player of the year. But off the field, things were not going so well for young Bill.

Bill was seventeen years old when his parents separated and divorced. He took it hard. And, as the only child still living at home, he took it personally. Not only did he feel lonely and isolated, but he also felt responsible for his parents' divorce. Fortunately, Bill's sister, Barbara, acted as a sounding board and helped keep him emotionally balanced. Barbara also bought Bill a dog, a rottweiler he named Rocky. Rocky became Bill's best friend.

The Road to Wrestling

Soon Bill was off to college. He could have played football at just about any college in the country. He could have gone to the University of Oklahoma and played for famed coach Barry Switzer, as so many outstanding athletes had chosen to do. But like his brothers, Bill decided to go to college out of state. He accepted a football scholarship from the University of Georgia and became a Georgia Bulldog.

Goldberg made an immediate impact on the Bulldogs' famed "Dawg Pound." He was an intimidating player who walked with a swagger. Between 1987 and 1989, he was a two-time All-Southeast Conference defender. His 348 tackles during his college career placed him seventh on the school's all-time great players list. During his senior year, he set a school record with 121 tackles. He was eventually named to Georgia's all-decade team of the 1980s.

"He was always a great competitor," Georgia coach Vince Dooley said. "He's a relentless athlete who would hit you so hard your teeth would shake." Goldberg graduated with a degree in psychology from the University of Georgia and prepared to move onto the next step: a career in the National Football League (NFL). During his senior year, Bill had been ranked among the top fifty-two college players in the nation. His prospects of being chosen by an NFL team looked bright.

The Road to Wrestling

Sadly, shortly before the NFL Combine, in which NFL coaches gather to watch the top college players, Goldberg came down with mononucleosis. His weight dropped from 279 to 245 pounds. He could not attend the combine, and ended up drafted later in the eleventh round by the Los Angeles Rams.

Goldberg's bad luck continued. That fall, in the Rams' final preseason game, he suffered a torn hamstring. The Rams cut him from their roster. Refusing to abandon his dream of playing pro football, Goldberg decided to play for the Sacramento Surge of the World League. While helping the Surge win the 1992 World League of American Football Championship, scouts

With his imposing build and sheer athletic prowess, Bill Goldberg was a natural when it came to professional wrestling.

The Road to Wrestling

for the NFL's Atlanta Falcons decided to sign him to the team.

With his playing weight back up to 270 pounds, Goldberg felt healthy. He also had some good times with the Falcons. He played fourteen games in three seasons for the Falcons. He was having his best season in 1994 until he suffered a torn abdominal muscle. Afraid of losing his job, Goldberg wrapped the muscle and played in pain for the rest of the season.

During the off-season, he underwent surgery to repair the tear. But the Falcons feared the injury was too serious to take a chance on his future. They did not protect him from the expansion draft, in which the two new teams in the league would pick players from the existing teams. The Carolina Panthers drafted Goldberg, but the injury did not heal. With a heavy heart, Goldberg retired from football, unwilling to compete if he could not give 100 percent.

"I did a lot of soul-searching," Goldberg told *Pro Wrestling Illustrated*. During his three seasons in Atlanta, Goldberg had met several competitors from the locally based World Championship Wrestling (WCW). After retiring, he worked as a personal trainer at a few Atlanta-area gyms and hung out with several WCW superstars, including Lex Luger, Sting, and Diamond Dallas Page. Goldberg had never been a big wrestling fan, having always concentrated on football, but the sport

The Road to Wrestling

interested him. He enjoyed watching World Class Wrestling and the Ultimate Wrestling Federation, and he admired the ring exploits of Bruiser Brody, Mil Mascaras, Jimmy Snuka—all large, agile wrestlers.

"Here and there on Saturdays, I saw wrestling matches on TV," Goldberg said. "But they weren't as interesting for me as football. I dreamed of playing football."

Noting Goldberg's size and athletic ability, Sting and Luger encouraged him to wrestle, bringing him to his first wrestling match. Goldberg met with WCW vice-president Eric Bischoff, who convinced him to give wrestling a try. "I'm not going to be some jerk thrown around the ring for 500 bucks," he told Bischoff. "I'm going to

Sparks fly during Goldberg's theatrical procession to the wrestling ring.

come in and I'm going to do it right, and I'm going to shoot the bull with you straight."

Goldberg signed with WCW in September 1996 and began training at WCW's Power Plant under Dwayne Bruce and wrestling legend Arn Anderson. He studied tapes of wrestling and martial arts such as sambo, a Russian combat technique that employs self-defense without weapons, and jujitsu, a martial art that uses an enemy's strength against him or her. Already, Goldberg was showing the same intensity and killer instinct in the wrestling ring that he had always shown on the football field.

2 The Winning Streak

September 22, 1997. E Arena in Salt Lake City, Utah. The event was a live broadcast of WCW's *Monday Nitro*, a weekly wrestling card, and the big crowd was there to see United States champion Curt Hennig battle Jeff Jarrett, Booker T face off against Scott Norton and Konnan in a handicap match, and Randy Savage battle Stevie Richards.

But as the combatants walked out to the ring for the second match of the

An opponent braces himself for impact as Goldberg dominates him during a ringside brawl.

night, the fans focused on the rookie making his professional wrestling debut: Bill Goldberg.

This guy looks familiar, thought many fans. Indeed, Goldberg bore a striking resemblance to wrestling superstar Steve Austin, who was extremely popular in a rival wrestling league, the World Wrestling Federation (WWF). Goldberg and Austin were of similar size. Austin was six feet two and 252 pounds. Goldberg was six feet four and 285 pounds.

They both had muscular, powerful-looking builds. They both sported intense gazes. And both were bald! The fans wondered, "Is this WCW's answer to Austin?"

Goldberg did nothing to stop the comparisons when he made short work of his opponent, veteran grappler Hugh Morrus. It was an impressive ring debut. "We have the same hairdo, that's all," Goldberg said of Austin.

One week later on *Nitro* in Worcester, Massachusetts, Goldberg's opponent was Barbarian, a huge, powerful man at six feet five and 295 pounds.

Goldberg destroyed him, and the fans were impressed.

With his parents watching on television or from the stands, Goldberg piled up one victory after another. He pinned Scotty Riggs on *Nitro* in Tampa, Florida, on October 13. Both his mother and father had been against their son becoming a pro wrestler, but Goldberg was quickly convincing them that he had made the right decision.

"When I told them I was starting a new career in the ring, they thought I lost it," Goldberg said. "But they knew that if I came to a certain conclusion, it was after doubts and considerations. I made it clear I don't intend to be just a wrestler."

The referee raises Goldberg's arm in victory following another pinfall.

The Winning Streak

Powerful, ruthless, and intense, Goldberg was becoming an overnight sensation. His first feud was with another football player, Steve "Mongo" McMichael. The former Chicago Bears great had prided himself on being the dominant former football player in WCW. Goldberg wanted to prove otherwise.

At Halloween Havoc in Las Vegas, on October 26, 1997, Goldberg interfered in McMichael's match against Alex Wright, resulting in a victory for Wright. After the match, McMichael's estranged wife Debra further infuriated him by giving Goldberg McMichael's Super Bowl ring.

Goldberg and McMichael were scheduled to meet at the World War III match in Auburn Hills, Michigan, on November 23, 1997. Before the match, McMichael attacked Goldberg with a lead pipe in the dressing-room area, injuring Goldberg and forcing him to back out of the match. Although Goldberg was still suffering from a groin injury and from the effects of the McMichael attack, he managed to pin McMichael at Starrcade '97 on December 28 in Washington, DC. The victory vaulted Goldberg onto WCW's list of top ten wrestlers, at number ten.

Goldberg was a human wrecking ball and piled up easy victories over a variety of opponents, including Barry Horowitz, Jerry Flynn, Chavo Guerrero Jr., Stevie Ray, Kendall Windham, Mike

The Winning Streak

Toldberg, Brad Armstrong, Meng, Mark Starr, Jim Powers, and Disco Inferno. Opponents feared his jackhammer and spear, a football-like combination move in which Goldberg slammed into his opponent's midsection. Through these moves, Goldberg had found an effective and devastating way to combine football and wrestling.

The fans, however, did not know what to think about Goldberg. This mysterious newcomer did not say much. He never smiled. Nobody knew if he was a rulebreaker or a fan favorite. The fans started booing him, thinking he was not showing them the proper respect. A rumor circulated that Goldberg was going to join the New World Order (NWO), the nefarious band of rulebreakers, led by Hulk Hogan, that was wreaking havoc on WCW. When Goldberg announced that he did not want to join the NWO, the fans started siding with him.

"Goldberg! Goldberg!" chanted the fans at his matches. Goldberg was becoming "Da Man." The Goldberg steamroller rolled on. He pinned Sick Boy on *Nitro* on March 2, 1998, in Philadelphia. He scored two victories over Yuji Nagata in three nights. Most of his matches lasted less than two minutes. WCW announcers started keeping track of Goldberg's winning streak; since making his debut, he had not lost once.

When Goldberg declared war on the NWO on *Thunder*, a broadcast wrestling competition, on March 19, 1998, the fans were squarely on his side.

However, Goldberg was not without his critics. Many experts claimed that Goldberg was not a wrestler, but a kicker and puncher, a brawler with few wrestling skills. "You've seen one Goldberg match, you've seen them all," went the typical criticism. Ironically, many people said the same thing about the NWO's Hogan.

"I could not care less what these people say," Goldberg replied. "They are probably guys who never stepped in the ring. They are probably people who don't have a lick of talent. They are probably people who didn't get that shot. You know what? I'll be the first one to admit it. I was a one-in-a-million shot. But they want me to be remorseful about it? Absolutely not!"

There was no reason to feel remorse, not when he was winning matches, gaining fans at a record-breaking clip, and garnering recognition as a wrestler to be reckoned with. In April 1998, WCW announced that Goldberg would wrestle the winner of the United States title bout between Raven and Diamond Dallas Page (DDP) at Spring Stampede. The match would take place on April 19, 1998, in Denver. The U.S. title is the second most important championship in WCW. Raven won the belt from DDP, and the next night

The Winning Streak

took on Goldberg on *Nitro* in Colorado Springs, Colorado.

Raven was a rulebreaker who loved to cheat and use foreign objects as weapons. Raven was the leader of the Flock, a group of wrestlers whose every move he controlled. But when the Flock interfered and attacked Goldberg, Da Man fought them off. Then he used his jackhammer and spear combination to pin Raven, whose U.S. title reign lasted only one day. Goldberg was a rookie champion.

Goldberg's winning streak soared to one hundred matches. In fact, he had become so popular that fans were chanting his name even when he wasn't on the card. When he wrestled on *Nitro* or *Thunder*, the television cameras followed him step-by-step as he made his way from the locker room to the ring, giving fans a peek at his single-minded intensity and focus. Nothing could distract Da Man.

Goldberg had a chance to prove himself against one of the all-time greats on June 13, 1998, at the Palumbo Center in Pittsburgh. After beating Konnan, Goldberg called out Sting, who waited in the locker room. Sting, a four-time WCW world heavyweight champion, accepted the challenge. But one minute into their match, members of Raven's Flock interfered and attacked both Sting and Goldberg. With Sting weakened, Goldberg beat him with a jackhammer. After the

Four-time WCW champ Sting, pictured here, was one of the many capable and respected opponents whom Goldberg defeated.

victory, Goldberg raised Sting's hand and helped him back to the locker room.

"I have the highest respect for Sting," Goldberg said, further endearing himself to the fans. "You're not gonna hear Bill Goldberg talking trash about Sting. I just wish the Flock would have stayed out of my business. I wanted Sting at 100 percent."

Goldberg thwarted challenges to his U.S. title from Perry Saturn and Konnan. He was a one-man wrecking crew whose victories had become so methodical that he started asking, "Who's next?" Of course, he was not asking for the name of his next opponent. He was asking for the name of his next victim.

The Champion 3

Very few statistics are kept in professional wrestling, so nobody knew whether Goldberg's winning streak, which had hit 106, was a record or approaching a record. More important, Goldberg had defeated Raven for the U.S. title. And Goldberg already had his eye on one goal: winning the WCW world heavyweight championship.

On June 30, 1998, J. J. Dillon, the head of WCW's executive committee, announced that Goldberg was the number-one contender for the world title held by Hulk Hogan. The match between Goldberg and Hogan was scheduled for July 6 at the Georgia Dome in Atlanta. Fans quickly bought up the 40,000 tickets on sale for the most eagerly anticipated match of the year.

Hogan, however, was not quite so eager. As the fans in the Georgia Dome tossed garbage and insults at him, Hogan told the fans, "This match ain't going to happen. But to show everybody here that I'm a fair man, I'm bringing in an NWO brother. He's going to give Goldberg his first loss tonight. Just in case Goldberg gets real lucky, then, and only then, will I grace you with my presence and kill Goldberg, 'Hollywood-style,' right in the middle of the ring."

Goldberg's opponent was Scott Hall, the six feet eight, 290-pound cofounder of the NWO. When the bell rang, an angry Goldberg shoved Hall to the mat. The two big men pushed and shoved each other, but Goldberg frustrated Hall and kept him off balance. Several NWO members, joined by several pro-WCW wrestlers, came ringside. As the NWO and WCW wrestlers brawled, Hall clotheslined Goldberg, who got right back up and flipped Hall to the mat. Goldberg used his jackhammer and spear combination to score the pin.

An hour later, Hogan and Goldberg stepped into the ring for their world title bout. Goldberg caught Hogan in a headlock. Hogan kicked and punched his way out, then scratched Goldberg and whipped him with the world title belt. Goldberg was in pain, but he grabbed the belt from Hogan and threw it out of the ring. Hogan, realizing he was in trouble, stepped out of the ring for a breather, then came back in and tossed Goldberg out of the ring to the arena floor.

Da Man was in trouble. Hogan smashed Goldberg's head against the metal barrier separating the fans from the ring. Goldberg staggered in pain. Hogan grabbed a chair and bashed Goldberg

The Champion

over the head three times. The fans could not believe what they were watching. Was the winning streak about to end?

When the action returned to the ring, Hogan continued the punishment by bodyslamming Goldberg to the mat. Then he scored with three consecutive legdrops, in which he leapt into the air and came down hard on Goldberg's body with an outstretched leg. Goldberg was all but finished.

Curt Hennig, a member of the NWO, walked toward the ring. Basketball star Karl Malone, who had been sitting in the audience, attacked Hennig, as Hogan turned to watch. That was a major mistake. Goldberg snuck up from behind Hogan and speared him to the mat. Then he lifted the champ high in the air and sent him crashing to the mat with a jackhammer. Goldberg draped his body on top of Hogan's. The crowd rose in anticipation. The referee made the three-count. Goldberg was the new WCW world champion.

It was an amazing feat. Only ten months after making his ring debut, Goldberg was the number one wrestler in WCW, and possibly the entire world. His detractors had been silenced. Goldberg had beaten every opponent who came his way. But, characteristically, he refused to gloat.

"Hulk Hogan has done more for the sport than a lot of people collectively," Goldberg remarked. "He's a legend. So, to

The Champion

wrestle him is one thing. To beat him is completely different. It's hard to describe the pressure that goes with being the world champion. Then again, no one can put more pressure on me than myself. Sure, it's a lot of pressure being world champion, but no more pressure than I put on myself."

Goldberg vowed not to back down from anyone. NWO members demanded matches against Goldberg. He beat Hennig with a jackhammer at Bash at the Beach on July 12, 1998, in San Diego. He beat the Giant (who had also won the world title as a rookie in 1996) and Brian Adams. Diamond Dallas Page and Sting, wrestlers loyal to WCW, also failed to beat Da Man.

Goldberg had nothing to prove or gain by entering the nine-man battle royal at the *Road Wild* pay-per-view special on August 8, 1998, in Sturgis, South Dakota, but he entered it anyway and eliminated five men, including Scott Hall, Konnan, Curt Hennig, Scott Norton, and Sting. Then he pinned the Giant with a jackhammer. Later in the card, Goldberg saved comedian Jay Leno from an attack by Eric Bischoff and Hulk Hogan. After clearing the ring, Goldberg shouted, "Who's next?"

Perhaps, "What's next?" would have been more appropriate. Goldberg was featured in articles in *Time*, *Newsweek*, and *USA Today*. Despite his success, he refused to rest. He added new moves to his repertoire and began wrestling at a faster pace. At the beginning of his career, he was always the aggressor, but Goldberg turned himself into a very good counter-wrestler. He had an answer for any move his opponents threw at him.

At Halloween Havoc on October 25, 1998, in Las Vegas, Nevada, Goldberg pinned Diamond Dallas Page in a high-spirited bout. Goldberg overpowered DDP. He also startled Page with several stepover takedowns and submission holds. DDP fought back when Goldberg injured his shoulder by crashing into the ringpost after a missed spear attempt. But another spear and a jackhammer

Goldberg and Diamond Dallas Page stare each other down in the ring.

spelled the end for Page and another victory for Goldberg.

On Halloween night, Goldberg put on his old University of Georgia Bulldogs jersey and ran onto the field with the team as they prepared to take on the University of Florida Gators in Jacksonville, Florida. The Bulldogs lost, placing the only blemish on Goldberg's sterling year.

Nobody else could touch him. When Chris Jericho started insulting Goldberg and calling him Greenberg, Goldberg used a spear to shut him up. Lesson learned. Goldberg was a man to be feared.

The Streak Ends

Goldberg had gone through a virtual obstacle course to win his first WCW world title. Even after being granted a world title shot against Hulk Hogan, he first had to beat Scott Hall, one of the most imposing wrestlers in the world. "If I had to do that, why shouldn't the next guy?" Goldberg wondered.

Goldberg prepared for World War III. One of the stipulations of World War III, a

The Streak Ends

sixty-person battle royal on November 22, 1998, was that the winner would receive a shot at the world title. Goldberg insisted that the match take place the same night.

"I had to go through two men the night I won the belt," Goldberg told *Pro Wrestling Illustrated Weekly*. "I'd like to see the same conditions honored at World War III. Just winning that battle royal will take a courageous effort from somebody, so let whoever wins get his shot right away. I want to face the best WCW has to offer as soon as possible. If my opponent isn't ready, I'll wait until *Nitro* [the next night], but that's as long as I want to wait. If the executive committee

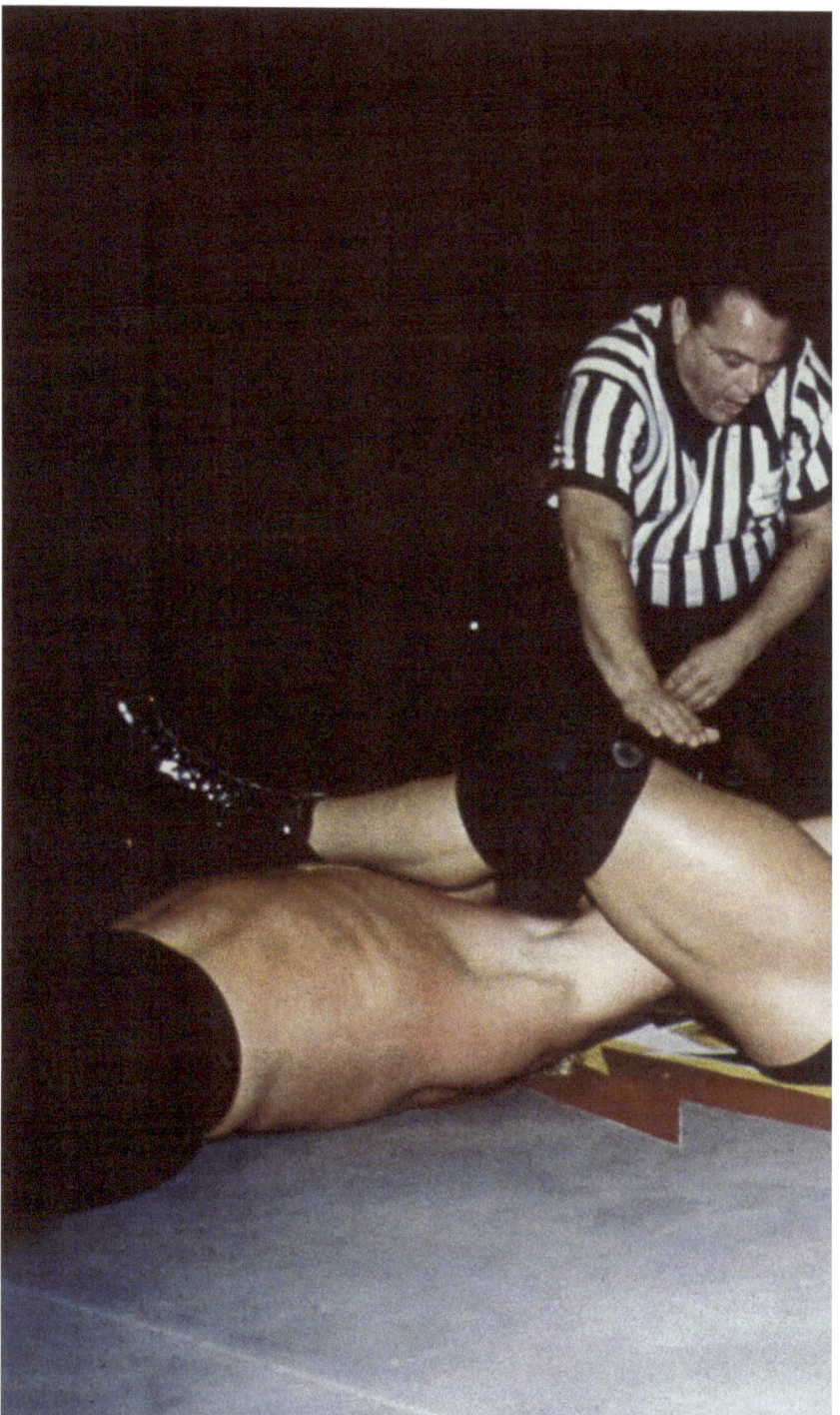

Another opponent falls before **Bill Goldberg's** relentless onslaught.

thinks I'm going eight weeks without a pay-per-view title match, they're crazy. I want to be known as a fighting champion. They can give me another worthy challenger at Starrcade."

Kevin Nash won the massive battle royal at World War III, but his match against Goldberg didn't take place the same night. The executive committee refused Goldberg's request and scheduled the match for Starrcade '98 on December 27, 1998, in Washington, DC. Nash was the leader of the NWO Wolfpac, which had separated from the NWO. Scott Hall, Nash's former friend, was still in the original group, known as NWO Hollywood (for Hulk "Hollywood" Hogan).

The Streak Ends

"I think Kevin Nash is one person who the fans would like to see me go up against," Goldberg said. "I ain't backing down, and I ain't afraid of anyone in this sport, or anyone in another sport, or anyone who walks the face of this earth, for that matter. There are a lot of people who think he will take control of me and give me my first loss, but I'm here to tell you that that ain't going to happen."

The winning streak had extended to 173 consecutive matches by the time Goldberg stepped into the ring at Starrcade. The fans wondered which wrestler they should root for. Both men were fan favorites. When the bell rang, Goldberg forced the action and backed up Nash against the ropes. Nash countered and put Goldberg in a headlock. Goldberg lifted Nash and slammed him backward to the mat. The two men brawled in an impressive battle, but neither could gain an advantage.

Then, out of nowhere, Goldberg speared Nash. Goldberg held Nash and prepared to jackhammer him, but Nash countered with a low blow. Goldberg collapsed to the mat in pain. Nash pummeled Goldberg, but he countered with a swinging neckbreaker, in which he wrapped his arms around Nash's neck and throat, and hurled him to the mat. Nash was flat on his back. Goldberg again prepared for the jackknife, a variation of the powerbomb, when Disco Inferno stormed the ring.

The Streak Ends

Disco Inferno had been trying to join the Wolfpac and wanted to impress Nash. Goldberg held him off with a spear. Bam Bam Bigelow ran to the ring, but Goldberg clotheslined him over the top rope. Then Scott Hall came out.

Almost everybody in the building thought Hall was going to help Goldberg. After all, the two NWOs were at war. Hall climbed into the ring. The fans waited for him to do something. Hall pulled an electric cattle prod from under his shirt and forced the prod into Goldberg's chest. An electric current shuddered through Goldberg's body. The champ fell to the mat, shaking from being electrocuted. Nash, who did not know Hall had attacked Goldberg, picked up Goldberg and powerbombed him to the mat before covering him for the pin. The referee made the three-count. Goldberg's winning streak was over. Nash was the new champion.

After watching Hall's actions on videotape, Nash granted Goldberg a rematch on January 4, 1999, in Atlanta. But when he arrived at the arena, Goldberg was arrested by police and taken away in handcuffs. Miss Elizabeth, the NWO's manager, had accused him of sexual harassment.

Nash, certain that NWO Hollywood was behind this, demanded a match that night against Hogan. But it was all part of a

Fans cheer as Goldberg flips an opponent over his shoulders.

ruse. When the match started, Nash lay down and let Hogan pin him for the title.

By this time, the police realized that Elizabeth was lying. Goldberg was released. He returned to the arena and attacked Hogan and Nash. Then, Lex Luger, who was supposedly a friend of Goldberg's, helped Hogan and Nash batter Goldberg. Fortunately, several former football teammates from the Atlanta Falcons jumped in and saved Goldberg.

With Sting injured and the new NWO bigger, stronger, and more diabolical than ever, Goldberg became WCW's leader in the war against the NWO. He was the natural choice. The readers of *Pro Wrestling Illustrated* magazine had

The Streak Ends

recently named Goldberg Rookie of the Year and Inspirational Wrestler of the Year.

Goldberg had also finished second behind Steve Austin in the balloting for Most Popular Wrestler of the Year and Wrestler of the Year. His world title victory against Hogan finished third in the voting for Match of the Year. When *Playboy* magazine asked college students, "Who is the best athlete alive?" Goldberg ranked twelfth on a list of 455 athletes. He tied with baseball star Sammy Sosa and football great John Elway. Goldberg was one of the hottest wrestlers in the world, if not the hottest.

But after going his entire rookie year without losing a match, Goldberg's second

Bill Goldberg

year in wrestling had already started with a shocking loss and an attack by the NWO. The question on everybody's mind was, would Goldberg suffer from the feared sophomore jinx? And could he start a new winning streak?

The fans got the answer to their first question at Souled Out on January 17, 1999, in Charleston, West Virginia. Although he was wrestling with a bad knee, Goldberg overcame interference by Disco Inferno and Bam Bam Bigelow to beat Scott Hall. Two weeks later, Goldberg beat Kevin Nash in Los Angeles.

At six feet three and 368 pounds, with a tattooed head and huge arms, former Extreme Championship Wrestling

(ECW) champion Bam Bam Bigelow was a monster of a man. He was known as the Beast of the East. He seemed to be the perfect match for Goldberg in size and speed. Bigelow got in Goldberg's face, interfered in his matches, and jumped him in parking lots and backstage. Time and again, however, Goldberg humbled Bigelow. The Beast of the East was no match for Da Man.

Goldberg was starting to wonder: Who is a match for me? He started looking elsewhere for challenges. On February 19, Goldberg was a guest on *The Tonight Show with Jay Leno*.

"Ever since I started, everyone always called me a rip-off of Steve Austin,"

Goldberg said on the show. "And I don't know what he's thinking, or if he's thinking. I'll throw a hundred grand of my money, Austin. Any time, any place. We can even do it in the back alley of NBC studios."

Austin responded three days later by saying that the two would wrestle "when Goldberg made it to the big leagues," and that he currently had more important things to worry about. In other words, the match was a no-go. Goldberg, however, never turned down a challenge.

On March 29, 1999, a sellout crowd packed the Air Canada Centre in Toronto for the first-ever *Nitro* broadcast in Canada. During the card, Canadian wrestling superstar Bret Hart complained

The Streak Ends

to WCW announcer Gene Okerlund about being overlooked for title shots, and he challenged Goldberg.

Goldberg responded by storming the ring and spearing Hart in the chest. But after the spear, both men lay motionless on the mat for several minutes. Then, Hart rolled over onto Goldberg and covered him for the pin. Hart then removed his Toronto Maple Leafs jersey, revealing a metal vest. Hart grabbed the ring microphone.

"I quit!" Hart announced. "I proved I'm still the best. I beat the top guy they had, and in such a clever way." The fans, however, knew that Goldberg had never lost a fair-and-square match, and

Goldberg makes short work of "Beast of the East" Bam Bam Bigelow.

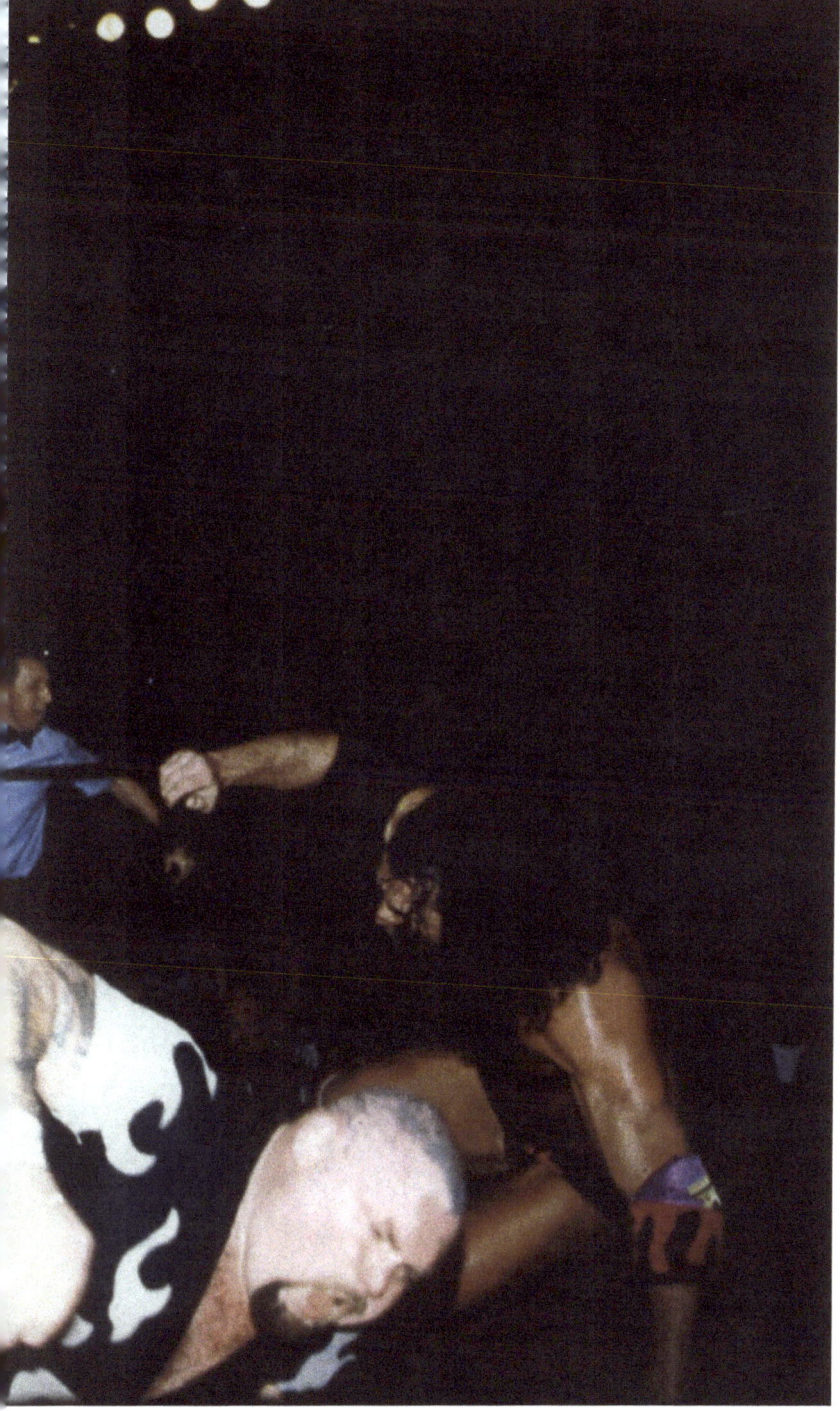

Goldberg knew it, too. At Spring Stampede on April 5 in Las Vegas, Goldberg avenged his first loss with an impressive victory over Kevin Nash.

But bad times were ahead. On May 9, 1998, at Slamboree in St. Louis, Missouri, Goldberg suffered a severely bruised ankle and reinjured his knee when Bret Hart attacked him during his match against Sting. A contract dispute with WCW lengthened Goldberg's unscheduled layoff. The fans chanted Goldberg's name, but he was nowhere in sight. At the peak of his popularity, Goldberg was on the shelf.

Ups and Downs

The fans at the Georgia Dome in Atlanta on July 5, 1999, received an unexpected surprise: the return of Bill Goldberg. Da Man came to the ring and yelled, "I'm back!" But he gave no indication as to when he would wrestle again.

Fans did not know that, behind the scenes, Goldberg was still negotiating his contract with WCW. But even during the main event, a match between Kevin Nash and Sid Vicious, the fans chanted,

"Goldberg! Goldberg!" Clearly, the former champion was still the most popular wrestler in the federation.

The contract dispute was settled in mid-July, and Goldberg celebrated his return to the ring with a victory over Diamond Dallas Page in Nashville, Tennessee. On *Nitro* on July 26 in Memphis, Tennessee, Rick Steiner laid out Goldberg with a chair. The following week, Sting and Goldberg lost to Steiner and Sid Vicious by disqualification. Vicious, a former two-time WWF world heavyweight champion, figured to give Goldberg one of the toughest tests of his short career.

"I'm not intimidated by anything Sid Vicious does or says," Goldberg told

Goldberg viciously powerbombs Diamond Dallas Page.

Bill Goldberg

The Wrestler. "I feel like I'm in the best physical condition of my life, and I'm just happy to be back in action, picking up where I left off. Now that the NWO has disintegrated, I feel like I'm more in my environment. I've never been one for sneak-attacks or double- or triple-teams. Just take the greatest wrestlers in the world: Hulk Hogan, the Total Package [Luger], Sting, Ric Flair, DDP, and me—and let the last one standing walk away with the world title. I know who it'll be and I think you do, too.

"What Sid has done in the past doesn't mean a thing to me. If I was going to get psyched out by someone's reputation, I would have choked against Sting or Hogan. Vicious is the classic bully. He built

Goldberg in one of many tag team contests in which he has wrestled.

up his winning streak by jumping people a lot smaller than he is. When Sid wrestles someone who can match his strength, he has no game plan. He starts making mistakes, and he leaves himself wide-open for a well-placed spear and a jackhammer. I'm ready for whatever he throws at me."

Vicious won the U.S. title from Chris Benoit on September 12, 1999, in Winston-Salem, North Carolina, making him the number one contender for the world title won that same night by Sting in a victory over Hulk Hogan. If Goldberg wanted to get back into world title contention, he needed to beat Vicious for the U.S. belt.

On September 18, 1999, in Louisville, Kentucky, Goldberg beat

Vicious by disqualification. Because titles can change hands only when the champion is pinned or submits, Vicious retained the title. They met again at Halloween Havoc on October 24 at the MGM Grand Garden Arena in Las Vegas.

Goldberg was a man on a mission when he arrived at the arena. He went searching for Vicious, found him backstage, and administered a brutal beating that left the U.S. champion battered and bloodied. Goldberg's attack served only to further anger Vicious, who showed no signs of injury when the match started later in the evening. Early on, Goldberg reopened a cut on Vicious's head. Blood poured down Vicious's face. The referee stepped in, stopped the bout, and declared Goldberg the winner and new U.S. champion.

But Goldberg was not done for the night. He then wound up battling Sting for the world title. Earlier in the card, Hogan had shown up in street clothes for his world title match against Sting and let Sting beat him. Not wanting to leave Las Vegas without a fight, Sting issued an open challenge to every wrestler in the building. All anyone had to do was show up for the main event. Only one man responded: Goldberg.

Sting was the aggressor, but Goldberg was the better man. Sting delivered three thunderous Stinger splashes, lifting Goldberg up and slamming him to the mat each time, but Goldberg jumped up and speared Sting in the middle of the ring. Then Goldberg scored with his jackhammer to win the match in just over three minutes. Goldberg was the U.S. and world heavyweight champion, or so it seemed.

Sting had a few tricks left up his sleeve. The next night on *Nitro* in Phoenix, Arizona, Sting convinced J. J. Dillon, the head of WCW's executive committee, that although he had asked for a challenge at Halloween Havoc, he never intended to put his title on the line. Dillon agreed, but he didn't return the belt. He stripped Sting of the title for attacking the referee after the match. The title was declared vacant.

Only a day after winning both the U.S. and world titles, Goldberg lost them both. J. J. Dillon had declared his victory over Sting invalid, and he lost his match at *Nitro* against Bret Hart. Interference by Vicious, Scott Hall, and Kevin Nash enabled Bret Hart to pin Goldberg for the U.S. title and eliminate Goldberg from the tournament. Goldberg's third year in the ring had started much like the second had: with a devastating loss. He was also not in contention for the world title. WCW decided that the world title would be decided in a thirty-two-man tournament.

Suddenly, Goldberg was losing matches in a way he never had before. On November 8 on *Nitro* in Indianapolis, Indiana, Goldberg lost a four-way ladder match against Hall, Vicious, and Hart. Hall won the U.S. title in the match. Goldberg defeated Vicious in an "I Quit" match—in which the loser agrees to quit wrestling for good—at Mayhem on November 21 in Toronto, then he did something he never dreamed he would do. On December 7 in Madison, Wisconsin, he teamed with rival Bret Hart to beat a tag team known as Creative Control for the WCW world tag-team championship. Their title reign lasted six days before they lost the belts to Hall and Nash on December 13, 1999, in New Orleans.

Hart and Goldberg were back on opposite sides of the ring at Starrcade '99 on December 19 in Washington, DC. Hart was the new WCW world champion, by

Bret "the Hitman" Hart often grappled with Bill Goldberg, but he teamed up with him for a tag team match once.

virtue of his victory in the thirty-two-man title tournament, and he had predicted an easy victory over Goldberg. The challenger, on the other hand, predicted that he would manhandle Hart, who was also known as the Hitman. It was a no-disqualification match, meaning somebody had to win either by pinfall or submission.

Early in the match, Goldberg slammed Hart to the mat. Goldberg clamped on an anklelock, which Hart tried to reverse into a sharpshooter leglock, a submission hold in which the attacker wraps his or her legs around an opponent and applies force to the thighs and lower back. Goldberg escaped, and the official referee for the match was knocked out as Goldberg and Hart battled in the center of the ring, and was replaced by a second referee.

Hart worked on Goldberg's bad knee and placed him in another sharpshooter. Goldberg reversed the hold, and the champion escaped by grabbing the ropes. The Hitman escaped Goldberg's sleeperhold and landed a series of body blows. Goldberg answered with some shots of his own, but he accidentally struck the referee.

Former wrestler Roddy Piper rushed down the aisle and jumped into the ring to replace the fallen referee. Just as Hart was about to place Goldberg in the sharpshooter, Piper called for the bell. Piper grabbed the belt and walked away. Hart chased after him. Piper stopped and handed Hart the belt.

The next night on *Nitro*, Piper justified his action by saying he thought that Goldberg had submitted, but the replays showed that Hart had not even applied the sharpshooter when Piper called for the bell. Later, however, Piper admitted, "My name is Roddy Piper and I sold out." His buyer: WCW executive Vince Russo. Piper's stunt was just an attempt by WCW to take a cheap shot at the WWF.

Hart, who a few years earlier had been robbed of the WWF world title under similar circumstances, told Goldberg: "You think I want to walk around with this piece of trash around my waist knowing that I didn't beat you soundly for it? Far as I'm concerned, this here world championship belt is vacant. 'Cause I don't want anything to do with it. I'll tell you what I'm gonna do . . . I'm gonna go back there right now, to the office, tell 'em to take this belt, and shove it right up their [butt]!"

The rematch was held later in the evening. During the match, Hall and Nash stormed the ring and clubbed Goldberg with baseball bats. Hart covered Goldberg for the pin attempt, but Piper interfered, tossed Hart aside, and covered Goldberg himself. Although the wrong man was making the pin, the referee made the three-count anyway. Hart had regained

Ups and Downs

the world title, but, even worse, the NWO was back and more dangerous than ever.

"'I've thought of Monday night a thousand times," Goldberg told the NWO three days later on *Thunder*. "Compassion is dead and so are you. One by one I'm going to rip your hearts out and shove them down your damn throats. It won't be who's next, but who's left." Near the end of the show, Goldberg grabbed a baseball bat and used it to smash the windows of an NWO limousine. But Goldberg caught his right arm on glass during the attack and shredded tendons in his right arm. His year ended with reconstructive surgery, and his future in doubt.

6 The Road to Retirement

There has always been more to Bill Goldberg than just wrestling. Since making his ring debut in late 1997, Goldberg has not only been a great athlete but a great role model, too. He always backed up his words with actions. He never boasted about his obvious greatness. He took each victory in stride and tried to improve after each loss.

The Road to Retirement

"My goal is to improve every single time I get in the ring," Goldberg said. "You're only as good as the next time you step into the ring. So, as long as I improve, then win, lose or draw, I don't care. My whole thing is to get better as a person, as an athlete, and a wrestler. If it means I lose here and there, if it means I don't get shots at the belts, so be it. As long as I improve, that's all that I am looking to accomplish."

His stardom inside the ring has resulted in increased visibility outside the ring. Goldberg appeared with Kevin Nash in an episode of *The New Love Boat*. He also appeared in the movie *Universal Soldier 2* with Jean-Claude Van Damme.

In addition to his wrestling, football, and television and film careers, Goldberg finds time to work for charity, including this appearance at an event called Kids Race Against Drugs.

But Goldberg is concerned with more than fame or celebrity. He is an active supporter of the Make-A-Wish Foundation for critically ill children and is a spokesperson for the National Humane Society.

"If you've got the public's eye and you don't do something positive with it, then you should never have had the notoriety in the first place," Goldberg said. "You should give back ten times what you get. I'm pretty big in the public eye right now. *Time* magazine. Leno. Regis and Kathy Lee. Whatever it may be, I'm trying to use those avenues to try to get to people on important issues."

But for all of his talk about doing the right thing, Goldberg was about to undergo a shocking change. The seeds of this change were planted on April 10, 2000, while Goldberg was still recovering from his arm injury. That night on *Nitro*, WCW executives Vince Russo and Eric Bischoff introduced a new era for the federation. The New Blood, a band of young wrestlers formed by WCW executives to create conflict in the league, were ready to make an impact. Their opponents, the Millionaires Club, were the established, veteran wrestlers.

For weeks, Goldberg's new monster truck loomed in the background on *Nitro* and *Thunder* as Russo's New Blood and the Millionaires Club battled. Everybody assumed Goldberg would side with the

Millionaires Club. But at Bash at the Beach on June 11 in Baltimore, Maryland, Goldberg drove his monster truck to the ring, speared Kevin Nash, and hugged Bischoff and Russo. The fans could not believe it—for the first time in his career, Goldberg was a rulebreaker.

One night later on *Nitro* in Richmond, Virginia, Goldberg explained the reasons for his turn. He was tired of the Millionaires Club stabbing him in the back. "Don't ask me why," Goldberg told the fans. "The question is, 'Why not?'"

The new Goldberg was more ruthless than ever. On *Nitro* on June 26 in Des Moines, Iowa, Goldberg beat Hacksaw Jim Duggan with a jackhammer and then

Bill Goldberg takes a breather while staring down an opponent.

punched Duggan in the kidneys. Duggan had to be taken away on a stretcher. At the end of the card, Goldberg pulled out Nash's contract and ripped it to pieces.

Who was next? Scott Hall. Goldberg called Hall and Nash "two big pieces of garbage" and claimed that he had carried the company on his back for two years but received no appreciation from the fans. It was the type of boast no one ever expected to hear from Goldberg.

Hall's contract was on the line at Bash at the Beach on July 9, 2000, in Daytona Beach, Florida, when Goldberg battled Nash. Goldberg tried to spear Nash, but Nash moved out of the way at the last minute. Nash got ready to jackknife

Goldberg, but Scott Steiner attacked Nash from behind. Goldberg pinned Nash, then ripped up Hall's contract. But the Goldberg-Steiner alliance did not last long. A week later, the two men came to blows.

Goldberg received a shot at WCW world champion Booker T on July 24, 2000. Goldberg attacked Booker T early in the card, but Booker T was ready for him the next time. Goldberg was attacked by both Jeff Jarrett and the Cat during the match, and he suffered a rare clean pin at the hands of Booker T. But afterward, Goldberg speared and jackhammered the champion.

But as fierce and violent as he became as a rulebreaker, Goldberg seemed uncomfortable in the role. As it turns out, he never really wanted to be a rulebreaker and had gone along only to help WCW's ratings. Being a rulebreaker went against everything his parents had taught him to be, and everything he wanted to be. Secretly, he despised Vince Russo and Eric Bischoff. He wanted nothing to do with them. He wanted to be his own man.

Goldberg's anger came to a head at the *New Blood Rising* pay-per-view match on August 13 in Vancouver, British Columbia. Goldberg, Nash, and Scott Steiner battled in a three-way match to decide who would be the number one contender for the WCW world title. Goldberg, however, was nowhere to be found when the starting bell rang. As Nash and Steiner fought outside the ring, Goldberg ran down the aisle and slugged Nash with a chair. Nash and Goldberg battled in the middle of the ring. Nash tried to set up Goldberg for a powerbomb, but Goldberg pushed him out of the ring and then walked out of the ring himself.

That's when Vince Russo walked down the aisle and ordered Goldberg to return to the ring. Goldberg refused. Nash went on to beat Steiner and earn a shot at the world championship, much to Russo's annoyance.

Russo threatened to fire Goldberg and offered to release him from his contract with WCW on the August 21 *Nitro*. Goldberg decided not to sign the release. Meanwhile, Scott Steiner had gone to the hotel where Goldberg was staying and kidnapped Goldberg's girlfriend, Beth. Later in the card, Steiner and Jarrett bashed Goldberg with a steel chair. Goldberg could not do anything but watch as Steiner placed Beth in a submission hold.

Goldberg was more popular than ever before. Steiner used a lead pipe to beat Goldberg at Fall Brawl on September 17 in Buffalo. The next night, Goldberg attacked Russo on *Nitro*, much to the delight of the fans. But Russo planned on having the last laugh. In one of the most diabolical plots ever conceived by a

The Road to Retirement

wrestling executive, Russo challenged Goldberg not only to restart but also to surpass his rookie winning streak of 176 consecutive matches. If Goldberg exceeded that winning streak, then—and only then—would he get a shot at the WCW world title. And if he lost one match along the way, his WCW career would be over.

Goldberg set out to meet this almost impossible challenge. He rolled up one victory after another, sometimes winning two or three matches in one night as Russo made the challenges more difficult. At Halloween Havoc on October 29 in Las Vegas, Goldberg overcame injured ribs to defeat Kronik. Then he confronted his biggest challenge: a feud with musclemen Lex Luger and Buff Bagwell, the duo known as Totally Buff.

Goldberg defeated Luger at Mayhem on November 26 in Milwaukee, Wisconsin. Goldberg scored with a jackhammer that sent Luger crashing to the mat and scored the pin to end the intense match. Luger, however, was far more ruthless than Goldberg could have ever imagined. Enter Dwayne "Sarge" Bruce, the man who had trained and been Goldberg's mentor at the Power Plant, a WCW training center.

On December 12, Goldberg was forced to wrestle Bruce. Goldberg did not want to wrestle his mentor, but Bruce insisted and Goldberg scored the pin following a gingerly applied jackhammer.

Five days later, at Starrcade in Washington, DC, Luger brutally attacked Bruce. Goldberg got revenge later in the card by pinning Luger in a vicious match.

But Goldberg was clearly distracted. On *Nitro* on January 8, 2001, Luger and Bagwell attacked Goldberg and Bruce. And at the *Sin* pay-per-view match on January 14, in Indianapolis, Indiana, Goldberg and Bruce squared off in a grudge match against Bagwell and Luger.

Goldberg assaulted Luger at the outset. Bagwell tagged in and scored with a suplex only to get pressed to the sky and slammed to the mat. Bruce tagged in and landed with an elbow on Bagwell. Luger and Bagwell, however, managed to keep Bruce on their side of the ring and wore him down with kicks and punches. Bagwell tagged in to Luger as Bruce tagged in Goldberg. Goldberg was enraged, and he unleashed a punishing assault on Luger.

But then something strange happened: A fan made his way to ringside. Nobody knew who this person was, or why he was there, until the fan sprayed Goldberg in the eyes with a can of mace. WCW security guards grabbed the fan. Luger pulled the guards off and gave the fan a high five. As a blinded Goldberg tried to rub the mace out of his eyes, Luger and Bagwell sent Goldberg crashing to the mat, then scored the pin. The

Goldberg mugs for the crowd while being interviewed by wrestling commentator "Mean" Gene Okerlund.

new winning streak was over, and so was Goldberg's WCW career.

Have we seen the last of Bill Goldberg? At thirty-five, Goldberg is at an age when many wrestling greats of the past were first hitting their prime. Despite the many injuries he has suffered, Goldberg still has the ability to be an intimidating, dominating wrestler, and a world champion, if given the chance.

But where will he get that chance? In WCW? Probably not. In the WWF? Perhaps. This much is sure: Wrestling fans around the world are hoping to see more of Da Man. Who's next? Hopefully, it's Goldberg.

Glossary

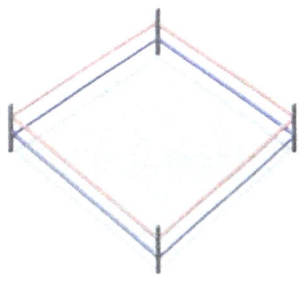

battle royal Match—usually involving ten or more wrestlers—in which the object is to eliminate your opponents by pinning them or throwing them over the top rope and to the arena floor. The winner is the last man standing.

bodyslam Basic offensive wrestling maneuver in which the attacker lifts his opponent and hurls him to the mat.

clothesline An offensive move in which

the attacking wrestler sticks out his arm and uses it to strike his victim in the neck. It is often executed by whipping the opponent into the ropes, then striking him in the neck on the rebound.

disqualification Ruling by the referee in which a wrestler automatically loses a match for violating a rule.

draw In wrestling, a match in which neither wrestler wins; a tie.

feud A series of matches between two wrestlers or two tag teams. Many times one wrestler will bad-mouth the other wrestler or will sneak attack the wrestler.

foreign object An illegal object used in the ring, such as a chair or a pencil.

jackhammer Maneuver in which an

opponent is hoisted up in the air while in a headlock, and then is dropped violently on his head.

pinfall A win achieved by a pin. A pin occurs when either both shoulders or both shoulder blades are held in contact with the mat for three continuous seconds. A pin ends a match.

powerbomb Violent offensive maneuver in which the attacker lifts his opponent, turns him upside down, and slams him shoulder-first to the mat.

spear Running tackle used by Goldberg as an offensive maneuver.

submission hold A move that makes an opponent give up without being pinned.

submission match Special match in which the only way to win is by forcing your opponent to submit.

tag team match Match involving two teams of two or more wrestlers. Only one wrestler from each team is allowed in the ring at a time.

For More Information

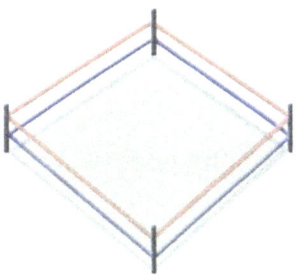

Magazines

Pro Wrestling Illustrated, The Wrestler, Inside Wrestling, Wrestle America, and *Wrestling Superstars*
London Publishing Company
7002 West Butler Pike
Ambler, PA 19002

WCW Magazine
P.O. Box 420235
Palm Coast, FL 32142-0235

WOW Magazine
McMillen Communications
P.O. Box 500
Missouri City, TX 77459-9904
e-mail: woworder@mcmillencomm.com

Web Sites

Bill Goldberg site
http://www.goldbergbook.com

Professional Wrestling Online Museum
http://www.wrestlingmuseum.com

Pro Wrestling Torch newsletter
http://www.pwtorch.com

For More Information

World Championship Wrestling
http://www.wcw.com

World Wrestling Federation
http://www.wwf.com

For Further Reading

Albano, Lou, Bert Randolph Sugar, and Michael Benson. *The Complete Idiot's Guide to Pro Wrestling*. New York: Alpha Books, 1999.

Archer, Jeff. *Theater in a Squared Circle*. New York: White-Boucke Publishing, 1999.

Cohen, Dan. *Wrestling Renegades: An In-Depth Look at Today's Superstars of Pro Wrestling*. New York: Archway, 1999.

Conner, Floyd. *Wrestling's Most Wanted: The Top 10 Book of Pro Wrestling's Outrageous Performers, Punishing Piledrivers, and Other Oddities*. Washington, DC: Brassey's, Inc., 2001.

For Further Reading

Goldberg, Bill. *I'm Next: The Strange Journey of America's Most Unlikely Superhero*. New York: Crown, 2000.

Hofstede, David. *Slammin': Wrestling's Greatest Heroes and Villains*. New York: ECW Press, 1999.

Mazer, Sharon. *Professional Wrestling: Sport and Spectacle*. Jackson, MI: University Press of Mississippi, 1998.

Myers, Robert, and Adolph Caso. *The Professional Wrestling Trivia Book*. Boston, MA: Branden Books, 1999.

Works Cited

"Bill Goldberg." *The Wrestling Analyst*, November 1998, pp. 12–17.

"For Goldberg, the Wrestling Ring Was His True Field of Dreams." *Wrestling True Life Stories*, Vol. 2, Winter 1998, pp. 76–86.

"Nash Wins Title; Bischoff Tops Flair at Starrcade." *Pro Wrestling Illustrated Weekly*, January 1999, p. 1.

Pearlman, Jeff. "Slam! Bam! Goldberg! Bill Goldberg Is the WCW's Hottest Star, but He's Still Bitter About His NFL Career." *Sports Illustrated*, April 19, 1999, p. 7.

"Supercards '98." *Pro Wrestling Illustrated*, August 1998, pp. 19–24.

Index

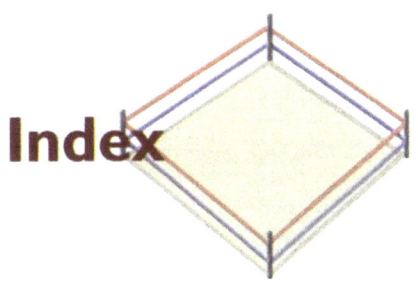

A
Atlanta Falcons, 13, 14, 54
Austin, Steve, 19–20, 55, 57–58

B
Bagwell, Buff, 94, 95–96
Bash at the Beach, 39, 86, 88
battle royals, 40, 45, 48
Bigelow, Bam Bam, 51, 56, 57
Bischoff, Eric, 15, 40, 85, 86, 90
Booker T, 18, 89
Bruce, Dwayne, 17, 94–96

D
Dillon, J. J., 34, 71, 72
Disco Inferno, 25, 50–51, 56
Duggan, Hacksaw Jim, 86–88

E
Edison High School (Tulsa, OK), 6, 7, 8
Elizabeth, Miss, 52, 54
Extreme Championship Wrestling (ECW), 56–57

F
Flock, the, 29, 30, 32

G

Georgia Bulldogs, 9, 43
Giant, the, 39, 40
Goldberg, Bill
  childhood, 5–8
  in college, 9–11
  family, 5–6, 7, 8, 21, 90
  and football, 6–8
    9–14, 15, 17, 25
    43, 54
  injuries, 11, 13–14, 24,
    41, 62, 79, 85,
    93, 98
  retirement from
    wrestling, 98
  as role model, 80, 84
  as rulebreaker, 86
    90–91
  size/appearance, 7,
    11, 13, 15, 20
  start of wrestling
    career, 14–17, 19, 21
  television/movie
    appearances,
    57–58, 81
  winning streak,
    26–27, 29, 33, 49
    52, 55–56, 93, 98

H

Hall, Scott, 35, 40, 44, 48,
  51–52, 56, 72–73,
  78, 88, 89
Halloween Havoc, 23, 41,
  69, 71, 93
Hart, Bret, 58–59, 62, 72,
  73–79
Hennig, Curt, 18, 37, 39, 40
Hogan, Hulk, 5, 26, 27,
  34–35, 36–39, 40, 44,
  48, 52–54, 55, 66,
  68, 70

J

Jarrett, Jeff, 18, 89, 92
jujitsu, 17

K

Konnan, 18, 30, 32, 40

L

Leno, Jay, 40, 57, 84

Index

Luger, Lex, 14, 15, 54, 66, 94, 95–96

M
Malone, Karl, 37
McMichael, Steve "Mongo," 23–34
Millionaires Club, 85–86
Monday Nitro, 18, 20, 21, 26, 29, 45, 58, 64, 71, 72, 77, 85, 86, 92, 95

N
Nash, Kevin, 48–54, 56, 62, 63, 72, 73, 78, 81, 86, 88–89, 90–91
National Football League (NFL), 10, 11, 13
New Blood, the, 85
New World Order (NWO), 26, 27, 34–35, 37, 39 48, 51, 52, 54, 56 66, 79
  NWO Hollywood, 48, 52
  NWO Wolfpac, 48, 51
Norton, Scott, 18, 40

P
Page, Diamond Dallas, 5, 14, 28, 39, 41–43, 64, 66
Piper, Roddy, 76–77, 78
Power Plant, the, 17, 94
Pro Wrestling Illustrated, 14, 54–55
Pro Wrestling Illustrated Weekly, 45

R
Raven, 28–29, 30, 33
Russo, Vince, 77, 85, 86, 90, 91–93

S
sambo, 17
Spring Stampede, 28, 62
Starrcade, 24, 48, 49, 73, 95
Steiner, Scott, 89, 90–91, 92
Sting, 5, 14, 15, 30–32, 39, 40, 54, 62, 64, 66, 68, 70–71, 72

T
tag teams, 27, 73, 95

Thunder, 27, 29, 79, 85
title bouts, 28–29, 32, 33, 34, 36–38, 39, 44, 45, 48, 49–52, 54, 55, 59, 69–79

U
University of Georgia, 9–10, 43

V
Vicious, Sid, 5, 63, 64, 66–70, 72, 73

W
World Championship Wrestling (WCW), 14, 15, 17, 18, 20, 23, 24, 26, 28, 30, 33, 34, 35, 38, 39, 44, 45, 54, 59, 62, 63, 71, 72, 73, 77, 85, 89, 90, 92, 93, 96, 98
World War III, 23–24, 44–45, 48
World Wrestling Federation (WWF), 19, 64, 77, 98

Photo Credits

Cover and interior shots by Colin Bowman.

Series Design and Layout

Geri Giordano

www.ingramcontent.com/pod-product-compliance
Lightning Source LLC
Chambersburg PA
CBHW041219070526
44584CB00001B/11